Super Senses

Smelling

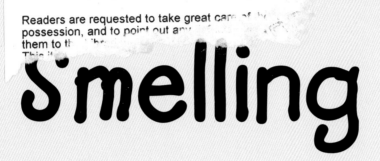

Mary Mackill

 Raintree

www.raintreepublishers.co.uk

Visit our website to find out more information about **Raintree** books.

To order:

☎ Phone 44 (0) 1865 888112

▤ Send a fax to 44 (0) 1865 314091

▭ Visit the Raintree Bookshop at **www.raintreepublishers.co.uk** to browse our catalogue and order online.

First published in Great Britain by Raintree, Halley Court, Jordan Hill, Oxford OX2 8EJ, part of Harcourt Education.
Raintree is a registered trademark of Harcourt Education Ltd.

Editorial: Kate Bellamy
Design: Jo Hinton-Malivoire and bigtop
Illustrations: Darren Lingard
Picture Research: Hannah Taylor and Fiona Orbell
Production: Helen McCreath

Originated by Chroma Graphics (Overseas) Pte. Ltd
Printed and bound in China by
South China Printing Company

ISBN 1 406 20024 7 (hardback)
ISBN 978 1 406 20024 9 (hardback)
10 09 08 07 06
10 9 8 7 6 5 4 3 2 1
ISBN 1 406 20031 X (paperback)
ISBN 978 1 406 20031 7 (paperback)
11 10 09 08 07
10 9 8 7 6 5 4 3 2 1

British Library Cataloguing in Publication Data
Mackill, Mary
Smelling – (Super Senses)
612.8'6
A full catalogue record for this book is available from the British Library.

Acknowledgements
The publishers would like to thank the following for permission to reproduce photographs:
Alamy Images pp. **13** (BananaStock), **17** (David Hoffman Photo Library), **4** (South West Images Scotland); Bubbles p. **9** (Loisjoy Thurstun); Corbis pp. **10** (Bob Krist), **19** (Tom Brakefield); Getty Images pp. **18**, **23b** (AFP), **14**, **23a** (Botanica), **12** (FoodPix), **5**, **7**, **23c** (Photodisc), **15**, **22** (Photographer's Choice), **16** (Taxi), **6** (The Image Bank); Harcourt Education Ltd pp. **20**, **21** (Tudor Photography); Science Photo Library p. **11** (Astrid & Hanns-Frieder Michler).

Cover photograph reproduced with permission of Getty Images/DK Stock.

Every effort has been made to contact copyright holders of any material reproduced in this book. Any omissions will be rectified in subsequent printings if notice is given to the publishers.

The paper used to print this book comes from sustainable resources.

Contents

Some words are shown in bold, **like this**. They are explained in the glossary on page 23.

What are my senses?

You have five **senses**. They help you to see, hear, taste, smell, and touch things.

Pretend you are in a garden.

What can you smell?

Smelling is one of your five senses.

What do I use to smell?

Most things give off a smell.

This is called a **scent**.

Your nose picks up these scents.

Your nose learns what different things smell like.

How does my sense of smell work?

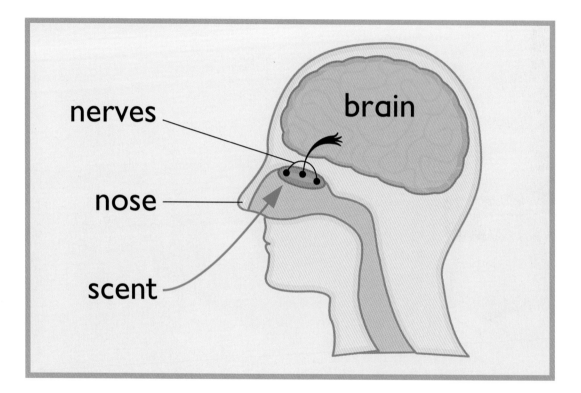

Smells come in to your nose and hit **nerves**.

The nerves send a message to your brain.

Your brain picks up the message.

Your brain would tell you that this sock smells bad!

What can I smell?

Trees and flowers have different **scents**.

Food that has gone bad can
have a strong, bad smell.

How does *my* sense of smell help me?

Your **sense** of smell helps you to stay safe.

Smelling smoke could mean that something is on fire.

The smell of food can make you feel hungry!

How can I smell things better?

Try to **breathe** in deeply.

More smells will come in through your nose.

Put your nose close to something.
You can smell it better.

How can I look after my sense of smell?

Try to stay healthy.

It is harder to smell if you have a cold.

Be careful not to **breathe** in
dangerous smells.

Animals have a sense of smell too!

Some animals have a very good **sense** of smell.

Dogs can find people by smelling their **scent**.

A skunk sprays a bad scent to keep other animals away!

Test your sense of smell

Hold your nose and eat a piece of chocolate.

Drink some water.

Stop holding your nose and eat another piece of chocolate.

Which piece of chocolate could you taste better?

Smelling food helps you to taste it better.

Your sense of smell is super!

Your **sense** of smell:

- tells you if food has gone bad

- warns you if something is on fire

- lets you know when tasty food is ready to eat!

Glossary

 **breathe** taking air into your body. You can smell things by breathing in through your nose.

 **nerve** part inside your body. Nerves work with the brain to sense things.

 **scent** a smell that is given off by something

 **sense** something that helps you to see, touch, taste, smell, and hear the things around you

Index

Note to Parents and Teachers

Reading for information is an important part of a child's literacy development. Learning begins with a question about something. Help children think of themselves as investigators and researchers by encouraging their questions about the world around them. Each chapter in this book begins with a question. Read the question together. Look at the pictures. Talk about what you think the answer might be. Then read the text to find out if your predictions were correct. Think of other questions you could ask about the topic, and discuss where you might find the answers. Assist children in using the picture glossary and the index to practice new vocabulary and research skills.